THE ADVENTURES OF THE COURSE KIDS!™

THROUGH FAITH AND GRACE

Helping Our Children Learn and Live Teachings from
A Course in Miracles

Barbara Franco Adams
B.S. Ed., M.S. Ed., C.A.S Ed. Admin.
ACIM Student

of **Course**
PUBLISHING
PENFIELD, NEW YORK

Illustrated by Animatus Studio
Fred Armstrong, Producer
Rebecca Share, Character Design
Emily Onyan, Backgrounds
De'LonWarren, Additional Illustration

Published by:

of Course
PUBLISHING
PENFIELD, NEW YORK

Portions quoted from *A Course in Miracles* are from the Second Edition, Foundation for Inner Peace, Viking, Penguin, 1996.

A Course in Miracles® and ACIM® are registered service marks and trademarks of the Foundation for Inner Peace, PO Box 598, Mill Valley, CA USA 94942

The Course Kids™ characters and scene backgrounds are trademarked, owned by and copyrighted by Barbara Franco Adams, 2014.

Disclaimer: Caregivers and teachers are reminded to use the contents of this book with the permission of the parents/primary caretaker of each child/student. In the case of schools, it is highly recommended that teachers receive the approval of their supervisors prior to implementing these readings and activities. The contents of this book are not intended to replace the formal religious practices or teachings of the family, but with parental permission, to augment them. As always, it is the prevue of the parents/primary caretakers to determine the spiritual or non-spiritual teachings and activities in which their children participate.

Table of Contents

Foreword

It was 11:57 p.m. December 31, 1999. We lived miles apart but were gathered together to share and celebrate hope, excitement, and the possibility for new beginnings. However, there was also fear. What would happen when the clock struck midnight? Would the economy collapse? Would we find ourselves without the essentials needed for existence? I stood with my family ready to toast and celebrate together whatever was to come. And then it happened. As I glanced at my six year-old daughter, I saw her face turn white and her eyes tear up. I knew what was coming. Quickly I picked her up, ran into the bathroom, held her hair back as we sat on the cold floor of a pink-tiled bathroom and rang in the New Year. As a mom of three kids, I had learned that nothing ever went as planned.

The very next day I began to study and practice *A Course in Miracles* (ACIM). With the dawning of a new millennium, I was asking the difficult questions. *Why am I here? What is the way to lasting happiness? What is real love? What can I offer the world? How can I be free of fear? And the most important question of all: What answers will I give my children when they ask me these questions?*

As I dove into the teachings of *A Course in Miracles*, I found the answers I had been looking for, answers that made sense, and provided the means to peace, joy and freedom from fear. But, how could I convey these teachings to my children who were still young? The answer was obvious. My children loved books. I would find an ACIM children's book that taught ACIM principles, captured (and kept) the attention of kids, and provided age appropriate activities that would help children have the experiences that I have had! I looked everywhere.

My search was futile... until now!

I am honored to be a friend and a witness to Barb's long standing commitment to inner transformation and healing. And I am very grateful to Barb for answering the call from parents and caregivers asking for a way to share what they are learning with those entrusted in their care.

Barb has taught all of us that it is never too early to learn the lessons of love and forgiveness and that children are ready and open to learn those lessons. She has heard their call because it is her own. And God has answered.

Thank you, Barb, for being God's messenger!

Patti Fields,
Spiritual Counselor, Teacher and Student of *A Course in Miracles*

Dedication

This book is dedicated to the adventurous spirit within each of us as we explore, remember, and at last celebrate our Oneness with our Source.

And, to *my* Course Kids™, Griffin, Emme, Jacey and Sammy whose unconditional love and joy provide me with a roadmap Home.

Who are the Course Kids™?

On their journey of discovery, the Course Kids™ are:

* **BRAVE** yet know when to ask for help
* **PATIENT** and willing to listen for the Answer
* **CONFIDENT** as they turn away from fear
* **LOVING** as they seek to join their heartstrings with others
* **STRONG** as they remember their Power Source

Introduction

When Jesus spoke, Helen listened.

Psychologist, Helen Schucman, wrote down Jesus' Words as she heard them in her mind. Dr. Schucman's friend and colleague, Dr. William Thetford, also a psychologist, believed in the messages that Helen was receiving and willingly typed her notes.

It was in the mid-1960s when Helen was first aware that Jesus was speaking to her, actually to both Bill and her, but Helen penned the notes. For seven years Dr. Schucman scribed Jesus' every word. It wouldn't be until 1976 when all of those words, now turned into chapters, would be put together into the book, which came to be known as *A Course in Miracles*.

Many adults throughout the world study the life changing curriculum of *A Course in Miracles*, but few children and young adults have had access to materials written for them so that they could be introduced to the powerful lessons of the Course. *The Adventures of the Course Kids!™ Through Faith and Grace* is one of the very first books, written by an educator and Course student, to bridge this divide and provide materials for children and young adults.

Now we are One with Him who is our Source.

A Course in Miracles W-pI.164

A Letter to the Parents

Dear Parents/Caregivers:

Children can independently read *Through Faith and Grace*, and the emerging library of *The Adventures of the Course Kids!*™. However the activities will be more meaningful for them if you, or another invested adult, support them in their inquiry and learning activities. It is ideal if this assistance comes from one who is a student of *A Course in Miracles* (ACIM) so that explanations and elaborations are in keeping with the Course's curriculum.

As our child's first teacher, we began nurturing their development from the moment we held them in our arms. We innately knew that by embracing them, talking and singing to them, we were building a bond that would form the foundation upon which, we could build a castle to the heavens.

> ***To teach is to demonstrate. There are only two thought systems, and you demonstrate that you believe one or the other is true all the time. From your demonstration others learn, and so do you. ...You cannot give to someone else, but only to yourself, and this you learn through teaching.***
>
> *M-Intro.2:1-3, 6*

As students of the Course, we want to pass on the valuable lessons that are positively changing our lives. We listen to the Words of our brother, Jesus and have a healing relationship with the Holy Spirit. We know that fear is the block to love, and that judgment is a call for love; yet another means of attacking our brothers and sisters. Through our learning, listening and releasing we've experienced miracles.

But with limited age and developmentally appropriate resources for children and teens, how do we help them learn these lessons so that they can experience miracles?

That's where I come in! As a Course student, I'm also a parent and grandparent. Additionally, I bring to the table my multiple years as a professional teacher, district and building administrator, trainer and educational consultant.

Teaching is my calling and before I retired I reveled in joyful repartee with my students. Active participation and a meaningful curriculum were the norm. (Just like the Course!) My students and I could explore the outer limits of their inquiries. What a joy it was to teach!

How much my students and I learned and grew together. How they filled me with their love. (I feel that beautiful emotion as I write these words.)

This is the background and experience that I bring to the writing of each of *The Adventures of the Course Kids!™* books. But I don't stop there. I have developed activities relevant to the story. I have provided teaching tools for you to incorporate into your role as a teacher so that you may more easily bring the lessons of the Course to life for your child. You'll find Suggested Teaching Techniques at the end of the story. In addition I have aligned *Through Faith and Grace* with a significant number of the Common Core English Language Arts/ Literacy Standards in Reading: Literature, Writing, and Speaking and Listening for grades 5-8. (This is the target group for which I wrote *Through Faith and Grace*, but the story will be enjoyed by 'children' of all ages!)

Should you have any reservations about your ability to guide your child through the activities provided at the end of the story, allow me to share a brief anecdote from *Absence from Felicity* written by Kenneth Wapnick, Ph.D., a friend of both Helen Schucman and Bill Thetford, and also one of those responsible for helping to organize the book, *A Course in Miracles.*

Bill was scheduled to attend a professional conference at Princeton University but did not wish to go. He expressed his fears to Helen. Soon after, Jesus sent this message to Bill through Helen. She scribed:

Bill, you can do much on behalf of your own (healing) and Helen's, and much more universally, as well, if you think of the Princeton meetings this way:

I am here to be truly helpful.

I am here to represent Christ, who sent me.

I do not have to worry about what to say or what to do because the One who sent me will direct me.

I am content to be wherever He wishes, knowing He goes there with me.

I will be healed as I let Him teach me to heal.

Absence from Felicity, p. 20

Perhaps, this prayer from Jesus to Bill will help allay any hesitations that you may have about being truly helpful to your child...and yourself. Remember, "I do not have to worry about what to say or what to do, because the One who sent me will direct me."

This is written with love from Barb

Let love replace their fears through you.

A Course in Miracles W-pI.199.7.4

A Letter to Course Kids™

Dear Course Kids:

I love you! I love your parents/caregivers! I love all of God's creations! And it is from this love that this story was born.

Get ready to read an exciting story because Faith and Grace are waiting for you. Through their tale, they'll share some lessons from *A Course in Miracles*, (which is sometimes shortened to ACIM or is just called the Course.)

Be an active reader as you move through the pages. Listen as Faith and Grace talk with each other. Watch as they interact with the people with whom they come in to contact. Hear what each character has to say, and think about what you would do and how you would react in each situation. Then ask yourself, "If I were Grace's friend, what kinds of things would I want to say to her?" or "What would I want to ask her?" Or you could ask, "If I were Grace what would I say, think, or do?" This is what we call making meaning from the text. Not just reading the words, but making the story come alive, asking ourselves questions and thinking about what it means to us.

This story is about a young girl whose mother convinces her to do something she does not want to do. Have your parents ever asked you to do something you didn't want to do? How did it turn out? How did you feel about that? Did you learn anything from the experience? Read to see what Grace learns.

At the end of the story, I've given you a glossary of terms from the Course and have provided you with their definitions. Then, I wrote a number of activities that I'd like you and your parent or caregiver to engage in. You don't have to do them all. You don't even have to do the activities in order. But read through all of them and see which ones call out to you. Start with those, and then any time you and your parent/caregiver wish, have fun with another activity. You'll be surprised not only with what you learn but how you'll start to perceive people and situations differently. I hope that you'll email me to share all of your insights at barb@ofcoursepublishing.com.

Okay My Friends, here we go. Open your mind and your heart as you begin your exciting journey as one of the many Course Kids!™

Love, your friend,
Barb
November 2014

Through Faith and Grace

"I don't want to go to that old homeless shelter, Mom. Those people aren't like us," said twelve-year old Grace as she helped her mother, Faith, clear the dinner table in their large suburban home.

"What do you mean they're not like us, Grace?"

"They're dirty, Mama. They smell and they're scary."

Like a vise tightening around her stomach, Grace sensed the fear building up again. The pain in the center of her belly and the light-headedness frightened her. Since her parents had divorced the world seemed as if it were spinning on the wrong axis. Grace felt unsteady and off balance.

Making her way to the refrigerator to put away the milk, Grace noticed the outdoor light above the redwood deck. She walked toward the two-panel, glass sliding doors that looked out over her large, tree-lined backyard. The first snow of the season had begun blanketing everything within sight. She admired nature's beauty. *It looks so safe and peaceful. I wish there was something that could cover me and make feel me safe and peaceful.*

With the sudden crash of a pot hitting the kitchen floor, Grace was jolted back to reality. "What was that?"

"Darn it!" said Faith. "Sorry, Honey. I lost my grip."

She watched her mother pick up the cookware. *I just hope I don't lose a grip on my feelings.*

Faith was almost finished loading the dishwasher. "So you think that the people at The Hospitality House are smelly and scary, huh? Sounds like you've been

listening to a lot of gobbledygook. I have to ask you, Grace, are you looking at your thoughts through the eyes of fear or are you seeing through the eyes of your heart?"

"Oh Mom, you're always saying things like that. I never know what you're talking about."

Faith took a deep breath. "Grace, you've never even been to The Hospitality House. You're just saying things because you're afraid, Honey."

"I'm not afraid, Mom. I just don't want to go. Why do I have to go? C'mon, Mama, I just want to stay home."

"I'm sure you do, Honey, but on Saturday, you're going with me to The Hospitality House where you'll meet some wonderful people, and I'm guessing you're going to learn a few things along the way."

Feeling her stomach tighten up again, Grace called out to her mother. "Please, Mama! Please tell me I don't have to go."

Aware of what her daughter was experiencing…again, Faith tried to keep the mood light. "C'mon Grace, just finish wiping off the table and save your energy for your homework. Now please hand me that last dish."

Faith Olson had lived in Springdale most of her forty-two years. The blond haired, blue-eyed, lawyer was well respected in town. She had met her husband, Patrick, in law school, where they had talked about opening their own practice. But Faith felt a need to follow her heart and wanted nothing to do with the "fancy-shmancy" legal offices in the city.

Instead, the social-minded lawyer felt a calling to offer her legal counsel to those who needed help the most, those in poverty. "I want to work for the non-profit organization, Lawyers for the People," Faith finally told Patrick.

He wasn't happy with her decision, and it was the beginning of the end of their marriage. Patrick wanted to make big money. Faith wanted to make a big difference in the lives of others.

Up since dawn, Faith was enjoying her second cup of coffee and humming a new tune that she had been trying to write for a few weeks. Gently, she strummed her six string blond-wood acoustic guitar, which had been one of her dearest friends since college. When it wasn't being played, the folk guitar was left standing in a corner of her room. But during times in which she felt emotions brewing inside of her, Faith would take hold of her beloved instrument and find comfort in embracing the warm wood. It was then that she'd strum the strings only to find herself composing a song. The words and the music flowed through her allowing Faith to release the stored up tension. With that she could feel peaceful and renewed but not now. The divorce had been difficult on the whole family. As much as she sought to make meaning of her music, today it wasn't going to happen. Grace's mother couldn't make the chords match her emotions. The song would have to wait.

Suddenly looking at her watch, Faith called upstairs to her daughter. She placed her guitar back in its holding place. "Time to get in the shower, Grace. We have to leave for The Hospitality House in about an hour. You need to get a move on it, Girl!"

"My stomach hurts, Mom. I can't go," Grace yelled down.

Knowing what a challenge this was for her only child, yet not wanting Grace to give in to her fears, Faith called back, "All you need is a warm shower and a good breakfast. You'll be just fine. Let's go, Grace. We can't be late. We have lots to do at The House."

"You're so mean, Mama!!"

"I know, Dear. Oh, and be sure to bring your sneaks. We'll be doing a lot of running around over there."

Standing frozen at the doorway of The Hospitality House, Grace took her first look into the soup kitchen where her mother had been volunteering for two years. "I can't do this, Mom. Really. I feel like I'm going to throw up."

"Grace, come and sit down here next to me. Let's talk for a few minutes." Faith lovingly guided her frightened child toward two folding chairs that were set up against a wall. "I want you to look around this room, Honey, and tell me what you see."

Grace sat in the brown metal chair and was silent for a few moments. She took some deep breaths before she answered her mother. "Okay." She breathed deeply again. "I see a stove, a refrigerator and a big sink." More heavy breaths followed. "I see some huge pots, a bunch of tables and chairs and an old TV."

"Now look at the people, Honey. Tell me what you see."

Grace sighed. "Mom, do I have to?"

"You can do this, Sweetie."

"All right." There was another moment's pause. Grace inhaled then exhaled deeply before speaking. "Over there is an old lady. Looks like she's falling asleep on the sofa. Maybe she's Mexican or something. It looks like she hasn't showered in a year, and her clothes and shoes are way too big."

The large room was painted a light green, and there were some pictures hanging on the walls that didn't seem to go together. A wooden staircase leading to the upstairs was in the far corner. For a brief moment, Grace wondered what was on the second and third floors. Then she looked to another area of this foreign place.

"Over there is a bunch of lazy people staring at the TV. They don't look much better. Some of them have really messy hair."

"Okay, what else do you see, Honey?"

"I see an old lady sitting all by herself in the corner. She's black, and it looks like she's missing some teeth or something. She's scares me a little."

Stroking her daughter's shiny brown hair, which was the same color as her father's, Faith gently coaxed Grace. "And back in the kitchen area, what do you see over there, Sweetheart?"

"Just some people chopping vegetables and a man stirring a big pot of something on the stove. There's a woman slicing bread. Most of them are white, and they all look nice."

"So you have made decisions about the people based on where they are in the room, what they look like, and what they're doing?"

"Uh, I guess so. I didn't think about it that way, but maybe I did. So what's the big deal, Mom?"

"Honey, you have invented the world you see based on your fears."

"I didn't invent anything, Mom. You asked and I told you what I saw."

"Grace, you told me what you see with your eyes. There's another way of looking at the world, and I know that you have the ability to do it. Look, Sweetheart, I'd like you to help prepare lunch for these folks. By the end of the day I want you to tell me again what you see, this time with your heart. And then, if you never want to come back here again, it'll be okay with me. I'll respect your decision. Do you agree?"

Grace rolled her eyes, looked at her mother for a long while and sighed, "You win, Mama. I agree."

"No Honey, it won't be just me who wins. Faith winked at her daughter. "Everybody will win."

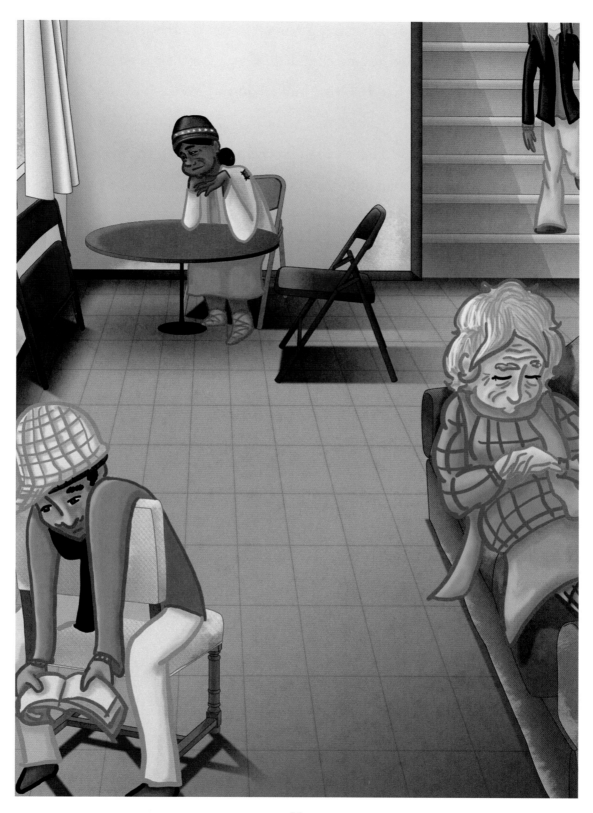

There was a lot of activity going on in the kitchen area of The House. People smiled at Grace but kept busy with their tasks. While she washed her hands, Grace looked down into the big metal sink with its rusting drain cover. She didn't want to make eye contact with anyone because then she knew she'd have to talk to them. But when she peeked a look to her right, she saw the man whom she had seen earlier stirring something in the old, huge dented pot. She now knew it was soup.

Grace thought he looked like a hippie. Noticing the way his long gray hair was pulled back with a blue and white bandana, she thought he could even be someone in a rock band. *And that brown leather belt holding up his jeans, well it looks like someone made it…maybe he made it. Hippies always make stuff like that. At least, that's what Daddy told me once. Of course he's a hippie, he's got a peace sign on the chain around his neck that's hanging over his tie-dyed t-shirt. That settles it: That guy's a hippie!*

"Would you mind peeling these carrots over here on the table, Grace?" the hippie asked. "Your mom told me your name. I'm Hank. This is your first time at The House, huh?"

"Oh hi. Yeah, this is my first time and I hope that it's my last." Grace scowled and began peeling the huge pile of carrots. They looked like they came right from a farm. *Probably a hippie farm!* The green stalks were still attached, the dirt, too.

"Really?" said Hank. "And why's that?"

"I don't like it here, but my mom's making me do this." The frown lines that formed along her forehead and next to her mouth were getting deeper. "She said that I'd learn some stuff. The only thing that I've learned so far is that I hate being here and I'm really, really tired."

"Sorry to hear that, Grace. I've been living and working here for twenty eight years, and I'm still not tired."

"Twenty eight years! You've got to be kidding me! What have you been doing all this time? Grace's once quiet voice now rose in pitch and volume. How can you stand it here? It's so depressing. And how can you not be tired?"

Hank added some salt and pepper to the simmering broth in the pot. "Wow, you've asked a lot of questions. Okay, let me see if I can answer them…one at a time."

"Well, each day I get up at 5:00 AM so that I can put the coffee on for the men and women who've been sleeping here at the shelter. The ones who've been sleeping on the streets begin walking in as soon as I open the door at 6:00 AM. That's when I start breakfast. Folks come to The House for warmth and a hot meal. They come here for a place that welcomes them, offers them hope, and doesn't make judgments about them. And about the depressing part, it's just the opposite, Grace. I find this work uplifting and joyous."

"Joyous?" Grace's expression changed from despair to curiosity. "How can you enjoy working in this run-down, old building in the middle of the city?"

"And, wait a minute, Hank. Did you say that you live here…at The Hospitality House? You're one of *them*?"

"One of them as in one of the many people who have been going through some rough times? Yes, Grace, I'm one of them. I live upstairs on the third floor." Hank pointed to the wooden staircase that Grace had seen earlier.

"Life hasn't always been easy for me." While he spoke, Hank continued to add ingredients to the soup: bay leaves, parsley, and diced celery. "I've had to work hard at finding peace." He spoke quietly and patiently. "And I'm one of you, too, Grace.

25

I'm part of your family."

Grace dropped the carrot peeler and took a step back. "What do you mean, you're a part of my family?" She started to feel a little a little light-headed again.

"Well, it's more like we're all part of the same family. So, all of us are connected, Grace. I'm sure your mom has taught you that we are all one with our Source. It doesn't matter what we look like or how we go through this life. We are perfect just the way we are, and in a not-so-mysterious way, our heartstrings are connected."

Grace took time out from her job and, for the first time, the lanky girl began to really listen to Hank. She didn't know why, but his words were breaking through her barrier of fear. *Mom says stuff like this all the time. But, the way Hank is saying it…well, it's starting to make sense.*

"What I do affects you," Hank continued. "What you do affects me *and*" pointing to the black woman sitting in the corner, "Miss Emma. Grace, it affects your mom and every other person in the room…on this planet. So instead of seeing a bunch of strangers, when you look around The House, see a family connected by their heartstrings. That's what we call seeing with your heart, Grace."

Picking up her kitchen tool again and peeling the carrots as fast as she was now talking, Faith's daughter had a look on her face that seemed to say, *I can't believe this!* "All right, now I'm really starting to get freaked out! That's exactly what my mom said, 'seeing with your heart.'"

"It's not a new thought, Grace. But it may be new to those who tend to look at the world as if they're always wearing sunglasses. Those of us who are aware of our heartstrings take off the dark glasses and see only the bright light of compassion and love."

Pausing, Grace began moving the peeler slower and more gently over the long,

orange vegetables. "I don't know about all of this stuff, but I've gotta back up, Hank. Did you also say that a lot of these people sleep on the streets? How could they? It's winter and it's freezing outside!"

The aroma of the soup was now beginning to fill The House. The smell of the gently simmering brew seemed to cast a spell of peace over the guests. Many were now talking quietly or were joined together playing cards or board games.

"Most of these fine folks are homeless, Grace, and the shelters in the city fill up fast. Once the beds are taken the rest of the men and women, and even some kids have to find shelter wherever they can. Some sleep along the railroad tracks. Others make their beds in old boxes they find outside of stores. It's a tough life on the streets."

"Why don't you just go live with your families like I live with my mom?"

"Lots of reasons. Sometimes we have no family nearby and other times our families won't or can't take us in. Some of these people are dealing with emotional problems. And for many of us there's just no work out there. The reasons are as many as there are people on the streets."

"Wow, I didn't know that. So you get up every day at 5:00 in the morning just to make coffee and breakfast for them?"

"Yes, for them and for me. And most nights I don't get to bed until well after midnight, not until the last person has left or has gone to bed. These are beautiful people, Grace, and I want to be in their presence. You see, what I give, I receive. When I give love, I receive love. That's how I'm able to feel so much joy working at The House."

As Hank was talking, Grace started to feel more at ease. She wasn't sure what it was, but his soothing voice relaxed her and her mind began wandering: *Is it his dark brown eyes that remind me of Daddy's? Maybe it's how calm his voice is while he's telling me all this. Dad is like that, too. I know! It's his half-smile. That's it! The right corner of Hank's mouth goes up just like Daddy's when he's talking and explaining things to me.*

Focusing again on Hank's explanation, Grace's mind started racing. She fired another question at Hank. "But aren't you exhausted? I'm tired after just a half-hour of peeling these dumb carrots."

"Maybe you've gotten so tired because your fear has dragged you down. It takes a lot out of you. Fear has a way of doing that, judgment, too. While you may have been judging these people by what you see on the outside, like their bodies, their hair and clothes, I see the light within each of them. I see with my heart and I feel the connection of our heartstrings." Hank paused a moment and looked directly into Grace's eyes. "I may be wrong here, Young Lady, but I'm beginning to feel like our heartstrings are making a connection. Am I right?"

Grace dropped her head slightly and broke into a...half-smile.

Tousling her hair with his big, work-worn hand, Hank winked and took a bunch of the peeled carrots from in front of his co-worker. He began chopping them on the dilapidated wooden table where Grace was working. Looking up, he noticed how the pre-teen was looking over at her mother, watching her every move.

"Your mother's a wise woman, Grace. You can learn a lot of lessons from her. Look at her over there. While she's washing the tables and setting up the chairs, your mom's talking with each and every one of our guests. Her heart has 20/20 vision and her heartstrings are connected to every one of us."

"And one other thing, Grace. Look at each of our guests as your mom interacts with them. They're either smiling or laughing or reaching out to join with her in

some way. That's just another example of what you give, you get."

The House was abuzz as the guests filed through the long food line. Sliding their metal trays along the serving rails, they appeared grateful as the volunteers warmly greeted them one-by-one, often by name. Each person took a helping of a cellophane wrapped tuna sandwich, a bowl of hot vegetable soup, and plate of homemade apple or cherry pie. Then taking their places on the hard metal chairs that were lined up next to the long, wooden tables, the guests immediately began to fill their stomachs.

After everyone had been served, and finally taking a break, Faith and Grace placed their food on a tray. At the mother's suggestion, they joined Miss Emma. The black woman, wearing a blue dress half covered by a patched white jacket, was still sitting off by herself at a little table in the corner. The second-hand ski hat that she wore to keep her ears warm covered most of her black hair.

"How are you today, Miss Emma, asked Faith. "May we join you?"

"Of course, Faith. I'm real good. Thank you for asking. And I'll bet that this lovely young lady is your daughter. Lord, she has your beautiful blue eyes."

"Yes, this is Grace. Turning toward her twelve-year old, Faith said, "Grace, I'd like you to meet Miss Emma. Miss Emma used to be a teacher."

Grace's eyes opened wide. "A teacher? Really, you were a teacher?" Her mind began reeling and thoughts crowded each other. *A teacher! Why would a teacher be in homeless shelter? Look at her ratty clothes. No teachers dress like that. And she's missing some front teeth. She can't be a teacher!*

"Yes, Darlin', I taught the babies." Miss Emma gave a broad smile. "Well, they weren't really babies, I just thought of them as my babies. At School #3, they were

31

all my babies. Praise the Lord, I loved them so."

"What happened? I mean…I'm sorry but, why are you here?" asked Grace.

"Grace!" said her mother. "That's a very personal question!"

"That's alright, Faith. I can see that your little girl is taking a step away from fear making her way toward the door of love. And if it helps her then it's worth it."

The middle-aged, ebony woman began her story: "You see, Grace, when I lost my husband and our only child to a car accident, I thought that my world had come to an end. I cried and I grieved for more than a year. Of course, I couldn't teach. I couldn't do much of anything, and I fell into a deep pit of sadness. Soon enough, I had little money to live on since my husband and I didn't have much saved up. Seemed like the sky fell in on me. I lost my house and pretty much lost the will to go on. That is until I remembered something my mother taught me, 'Let me be still and listen to the truth.'"

"What does that mean," asked Grace.

"It means that instead of letting fear run my life, I needed to be still and listen to God. You see, Precious One, by letting fear win, I was turning my back on my Power, my Strength.

Grace began noticing how well Miss Emma spoke. How she did sound like a teacher. In fact, and she didn't know why, but Miss Emma was even beginning to look like a teacher…whatever that meant.

Grace looked over to her mother sitting silently, eating her lunch … and smiling.

"Since God and I are one," said Miss Emma, "then the truth of the matter is that if God is strong, I am strong. If my Source is Love, then I am Love. If we are one with our Creator and with each other, then we never lose anyone, not God, not my husband and not my son. They are with me at The House. They are with me

wherever I am, Darlin'."

Hmm, thought Grace…*That's kinda like Daddy and me. If he and I are one then we are never apart. And, if Mama and Daddy and I are one, then we're never apart!"*

"That gave me my strength back and the will to take care of myself and give to others. That's the real reason I'm here, Grace. I'm here to share life. I'm here to share love. I'm here to teach again," said a proud-looking Miss Emma as she sat up tall with her ski cap tilted a little to one side.

"You teach here?" asked Grace as Faith looked on with an even broader smile.

"What do you teach? Who do you teach? Who are your students?"

"I teach about love," said Miss Emma. "I teach that, like you, I am the light of the world. With a big, tooth-gapped grin and her arms outstretched, Miss Emma continued, "My light shines for all to see and like a lighthouse, my light guides you Home, home to God." She then looked right into Grace's eyes. "Because what I know now is that all fear is past and only love is here."

"Wow," said Grace. "I'm the light of the world, too? I like that!"

"And you asked me who I teach, Grace? I teach anyone who wants to come and sit at my table," said Miss Emma with her face beaming. "Welcome to my table, Baby," she nodded. "You're my first student today."

Grace didn't know what to say. She just sat there, as if she were looking right through Miss Emma's deep brown eyes.

Faith watched and felt the joy well up within her.

"Miss Emma?" asked Grace. "May I come back next week and sit at your table again?"

After Faith and Grace helped clean the kitchen, sweep the floor and fold up the tables and chairs, they sat together on the old, partly torn sofa before heading home.

"Are you tired, Honey?" asked Faith

"I was before, but I'm not now, Mom. I feel good…and kinda happy, too."

Hugging her daughter and wearing a coy smile, Faith replied, "Well, isn't that interesting?"

Grace's mother went on, "So we had an agreement, Honey. You said that at the end of the day you would tell me what you see with your heart when you look around this room. Are you ready to share?"

Grace sat up tall, turned to look directly at her mother. "I think I am, Mom." She thought for a few moments and then replied. "I see a beautiful House that's filled with amazing people. When we first got here this morning, the place looked really dark and scary. Now it seems as though sunlight is shining through all of the windows, and outside it's almost dark! I don't know how that's possible, but that's what I see. You know what else, Mom? The people, like you who volunteer here, don't get paid any money, but you all seem to really love what you're doing. I think that's so neat. It's like you're getting paid with smiles and hugs."

Faith nodded.

"And Miss Emma. She's a really good teacher. When she was talking I felt, well… like, all good inside. I can't explain it. But, once I started listening to her and really looking at her, it was as though she was glowing. Does that make any sense to you, Mama?"

"It makes perfect sense, Honey, because, miracles are seen in light. And what happened with you today is nothing short of a miracle."

Faith made herself more comfortable on the old rundown couch. She drew her daughter close. "Sweetheart, you know that song I've been trying to write?"

"Yeah."

"Well, you just gave me the inspiration I've needed. The lyrics are welling up inside of me already. I'm going to write them down as soon as we get home."

"That'd be pretty cool, Mom! What's it gonna be about?"

"You'll see. I'll sing it for you when it's done."

Grace looked into her mother's gleaming blue eyes. "I learned a lot from Hank and Miss Emma today, from you, too, Mom. I'm so glad that you brought me here today."

"Me, too. You're welcome, Honey."

"Oh, by the way do you feel something tugging inside your chest?" Grace asked as she gave her mother a big hug.

"Huh?"

"It's my heartstrings, Mama. They're pulling on yours."

Glossary

A Course in Miracles (**ACIM**); **the Course:**
A spiritual path that guides its students toward finding happiness and peace by changing how we think about the world, others and ourselves. The Course teaches that love is the only thing that is true about all of God's Creations, no matter what mistakes we have made or what has happened in our lives.

Fear:
The emotion we feel when we expect to be hurt, when we are feeling a deep sense of loss, or when we are afraid we feel alone and separate from others. When we experience love we feel close to others. In truth, we cannot ever be alone or separate from one another, but fear gives us the feeling that we are separate and alone.

Forgiveness; to forgive:
The Course defines forgiveness differently than we're used to. Usually, we forgive someone after we've judged them or their actions as sinful or bad. We say, "I forgive you," but may not really feel they deserve it. The Course teaches that when we forgive, we accept that what we are seeing is a mistake and not the other person's reality. Because they are a creation of God, they must be holy. Therefore that can't really be the way we are seeing them. Forgiveness thus becomes our willingness to overlook the mistake so that we can see what is true. Through this form of forgiveness both people gain freedom. We are freed from anger and hurt, and the other person is freed from guilt. In seeing their innocence, we learn that we are also innocent. (See graphic, page 44.)

Judgment; to judge; judging:

We judge when we make decisions about others based on what we've learned in the past. When we make judgments about others, we are blind to their light and Godliness. When we are willing not to judge, we give up put-downs in favor of lift- ups. By not making any decisions about who they are, we lift others up in our mind so that we can see them in the light. A simple way to do this is to remember there are only two judgments that can ever be made: This is love, or This is a call for love. *(When I am afraid, I feel alone and without love. This makes me behave in an unloving manner. What I really want is to know that I am not alone and that I am loveable.)*

Love:

When we are willing to overlook mistakes and not judge others, we recognize that our true reality (Who we really are!) is love. Love is so valuable and attractive that when we are aware of it, we no longer want to judge or attack. We want to reach out so that we can feel love totally surrounding and embracing us. The Course teaches that when we experience Divine love, no matter what has happened, we love everyone in the same way and in the same amount.

Miracle:

(Read Perception, below, before reading this definition of a Miracle.)
Change your mind. Change your world! With the help of the Holy Spirit, we are able to change from judging others to not judging them. This allows only their light (love) and innocence to shine through. When the Holy Spirit changes our mind, He also changes the other person's mind. Now that's quite a miracle!

Perception; to perceive; perceiving:

Perception is the way our mind interprets what we are aware of in the world around us. We think we see the world with our physical eyes. But what we see actually comes from our judgments and fears. According to the Course, what we perceive is a result of what we think. Therefore we are not really seeing what really is there. The Holy Spirit can guide us in seeing reality as it truly exists because we are looking at the world through the filter of our thoughts. For example, if we feel afraid or are thinking in a negative way when we look at the world, we will see fear and negativity. (See graphic on page 43.)

The Holy Spirit; Spirit:

Most of us believe that we have separated from God, that we are not a part of God. We look at all of our different bodies and listen to our judging thoughts, and it seems hard to believe that we are really One with God. Because of this, God placed the Holy Spirit in our minds. Spirit guides us into thinking like God, and also helps us to see the Godliness or light in others regardless of what we think is wrong with them. All we need to do is ask the Holy Spirit for help in changing our minds about what we think and what we see. We hear Spirit's Answer by learning to quiet our mind. We quiet our mind by not judging. The Holy Spirit/Spirit is also known as (but not limited to) The Great Comforter, Universal Inspiration, the Healer, Guide, Christ Consciousness, Teacher, Voice for God, Communication Link and Helper.

Perception/Perceive

| Your eyes see... | ... a man. | Your mind interprets the man based on your fear and judgment. You might think, *That man is not like me. He's going to hurt me.* | Then you perceive the man based on your fears and judgments. |

But, when we let the Holy Spirit interpret what we are seeing, a miracle occurs.
People and situations appear a lot different in our mind!

| Your eyes see... | ... a man. | You say to the Holy Spirit, "I don't know anything. Please tell me who he really is." | When you quiet your mind, you can hear the Spirit's Answer, *The truth is that he is the pure light of love.* |

Forgiveness/Forgive

"I'm angry at what you did. You are a bad person."

I'll forgive you even though you don't deserve it. I'll make it look like everything is okay, but I still believe you are guilty.

"Thank you for forgiving me."

Why do I still feel guilty?

Why do I still feel angry and hurt?

... and how the Course teaches us to forgive.

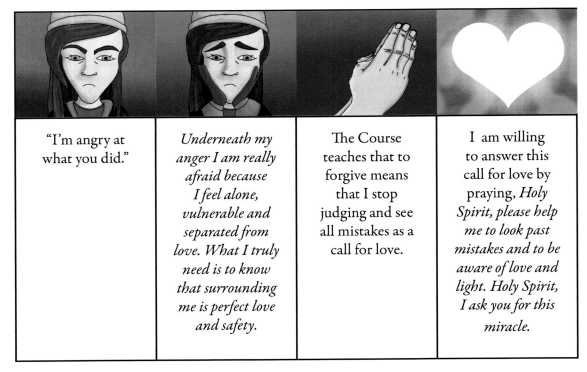

"I'm angry at what you did."

Underneath my anger I am really afraid because I feel alone, vulnerable and separated from love. What I truly need is to know that surrounding me is perfect love and safety.

The Course teaches that to forgive means that I stop judging and see all mistakes as a call for love.

I am willing to answer this call for love by praying, *Holy Spirit, please help me to look past mistakes and to be aware of love and light. Holy Spirit, I ask you for this miracle.*

The Course Kids™ friendly definitions were developed by Barb Adams and Patti Fields.

For Parents/Caregivers: Interacting With Your Child to Maximize Learning

Teaching is both an art and a science. The science of education is based on numerous years of research. Conducted in both controlled teaching laboratories and on-site classrooms, researchers have been able to determine, among other things, those teaching techniques that best foster learning. The art of teaching is more about the nuances and intuitions of the gifted educator who is able to plan as well as think on her feet about strategies that will engage her students in active participation. Many students thrive and are successful learners in both environments because they are provided with rigorous and relevant information. They are creatively challenged, while feeling respected, cared for (loved!), and safe.

As your child's parent/caregiver, you have the advantage of regularly providing a safe and nurturing environment. Your home exudes love and your bond with your child is a given. So, as you read *Through Faith and Grace* with your child and engage them in the activities that I've provided at the end of the story, how can you be most effective in teaching them what you'd like them to learn about the Course?

Like anything else, timing is everything. Choose a time and place conducive to learning. You'll want a relatively quiet environment when you're most assured of not being interrupted.

Set a positive, joyful tone by modeling your enthusiasm for reading and learning. Of course, you'll want to be patient as your child asks questions and moves from a familiar way of perceiving the world to that which is, at first, foreign to them. Remember how *you* feel as you sometimes struggle and then learn the lessons of the Course. Learning takes time and is accomplished by repeating a skill or a lesson multiple times. Be as patient with your child as the Holy Spirit is with you.

Move slowly and don't overwhelm your child. Let your child set the pace. One activity at a time may be all that he/she is ready to embrace

And finally, you are the one to set the safe harbor for the learning within your home. However, the true test of your child's comprehension will be demonstrated in the everyday, mundane interactions within your family, at school, and within the community. Like any other learning pursuit, you'll want to check in with your child from time-to-time to see how she/he is doing. Keep in mind that learning is a marathon and not a sprint.

Listed below are a few of the research-based teaching techniques that my colleagues and I have used successfully. I suggest that you read through the list and start with, perhaps two or three that seem natural to you. When you feel comfortable with them, add one or two more as you move through the learning activities with your child.

Suggested Teaching Techniques:

Link new information and/or skills to prior knowledge
Build on his/her background. What does she/he already know that you can build on? Move from the familiar to the less familiar or the unknown.

Wait time
The question-and-answer process should not be rapid fire. Slow down. By

waiting 3–7 seconds after asking questions, your child is more likely to respond with thoughtful, comprehensive answers.

Model desired skills and outcomes

Practice what you preach. In your everyday encounters, demonstrate how you incorporate the Course into your life. At an appropriate, private time, if your child seems receptive, engage them in a conversation. Ask them if they noticed how you handled a particular situation. Ask them if they observed a change in you or the other person. Let them know what your thinking process was as you moved through the experience. Share how you asked for a miracle and what you experienced.

Check for understanding

Use open-ended vs. closed-ended questions to determine how your child is connecting to prior knowledge and what she/he is understanding and learning. As much as possible, avoid closed-ended questions, those that require only a yes/no answer. Instead, ask open-ended questions like these examples:

* *Can you tell me about a time when...?*
* *How would you...?*
* *When could you...?*
* *Where would you go to find...?*
* *How did you feel when...?*
* *Who/Whom could you ask if...?*
* *How would you describe...?*
* *What do you think _____ was thinking when she...?*

Problem solving

Make this fun as well as challenging. Ask questions that allow your child to consider various situations where they have to think on their own and make decisions based on the Course. Some examples might be:

* What would you do if you were with a group of friends and they started talking in a judgmental way about another friend?

* You're feelings get hurt by your brother/sister/friend. How could you use the Course to feel better? And, what could you do so that you didn't feel like attacking (with words or actions) that person?

* If a new student entered your class and your first impression of him/her was that he/she was "weird," how could you use a lesson from the Course to have your perception of that new kid changed in your mind?

* Can you tell me about a real situation in your life that is troubling you that, using the lessons from the Course, you would like to problem-solve with me?

Model by thinking aloud

A *think-aloud* gives your child a window into your thinking process. They get a firsthand view of how you might handle particular situations. You can also ask your child to think aloud so that you can then discuss their process and any suggestions that you might offer. Also, be sure to honor their progress. Not all feedback need be critical. Acknowledgement of progress and success, as you know, are wonderful motivators! First set up the situation from something that you have experienced. An example follows:

I'm at the supermarket and this woman hits my cart with her cart. She has a screaming child with her and I find myself starting to get angry. Then, I remember that I can perceive this differently. **Think-aloud to explain your thought process:** *"Holy Spirit, I don't know anything. I have no idea what this woman and her child are experiencing. Please help me to see this situation differently." While quieting my mind, I receive the answer: I imagine that instead of perceiving the woman as mean and her child as annoying, I picture both of them as pure light. As I move through the supermarket I continue to think of them as pure light. Then, I notice that their light joins with mine. I begin to be aware that I no longer feel angry. In fact, when I think of them, I have a smile on my face and I feel love. "Thank you for this miracle, Holy Spirit!"*

To process the think-aloud, ask your child what she/he heard you say (Not verbatim but the essence of what you said) and what she/he learned from that experience.

For Parents/Caregivers and Children to Enjoy Together!

1. In your own words, either write or type what you think the book *Through Faith and Grace* is trying to teach you. Share it with your parent/caregiver and see if they agree. Discuss your differences and see if you and they can come to an agreement.

2. In your own words, explain to your parent/caregiver what the following words mean as they are used in the book, *Through Faith and Grace*. Then, ask them to tell you how they define the terms. Do you agree with each other's definitions? If not, discuss the points in which you disagree. Can you come to an agreement?

   * Miracle
   * Forgiveness
   * Perception
   * Judgment
   * Love
   * Fear
   * Holy Spirit/Spirit
   * *A Course in Miracles*

3. Write about a time when you and a friend were at the same place at the same time and later you each described it differently. (When you and your friend told each other what you saw and heard it was as if you two were in totally different places! How could that be?) Include what you learned

from that experience.

Read your story aloud to a willing audience. Ask for their feedback.

4. Demonstrate the following idea through an art form: *I am the light of the world.* W-pI.61 (Examples of art forms include: writing a poem, story, play or song; creating a painting or drawing; dancing, singing, playing a musical instrument; creating a sculpture, mobile, collage or any other creative way you can think of to express this idea.)

    Proudly tell about your masterpiece. Explain what it means and explain why you chose that particular art form. Ask for their feedback.

5. Cut out pictures from magazines (with your parent's/caregiver's permission) and create a collage that shows the following: *God's peace and joy are mine.* W-pI.105.

    Explain your collage to your parent/caregiver, and any anyone else who is a willing audience! Ask for their feedback.

6. Write a story or a poem with the following title: *I Invited Love In and Told Fear to Leave.* (Based on, *All fear is past and only love is here.* W-pII.293).

    Include within your story or poem: Why you invited love in and told fear to leave, and what happened because of doing this?

    Read your poem aloud to your parent/caregiver and anyone else who is a willing audience! Ask for their feedback.

7. Create a poster that you can hang in your room, or anywhere in your home, that shows this idea: *God, being Love, is also happiness.* W-pI.103.

    Explain your poster to your parent/caregiver and anyone else who is a willing audience! Ask them for their feedback.

8. Course Kids™ and Parents/Caregivers: Develop Your Own Activity!
   Create a unique activity that allows you to further your understanding
   of the Course. Remember to process it at the end of the activity. If you
   like, please tell me about the activity that you developed, at barb@
   ofcoursepublishing.com. If I'm able, I'll share it with others. For your
   privacy, I'll credit you by using only your first names. And if you want
   to share the general location of where you live (country, state, etc.), I'll
   include that, as well in one of the next upcoming books in the series, *The
   Adventures of The Course Kids!™*

And keep in mind, my Dear Friends: Miracles are not reserved for saints.

Afterword

Dear Course Kids!™

You know better than anyone that when learning is fun and your teacher expresses joy while guiding you through your lessons that you want to come back for more. And to top it off, when you're able to actually live what you learn...you've achieved amazing success!

As one of the Course Kids™, your job now is to live your lessons! Your life can be an exciting adventure as you start to see with your heart and connect with your heartstrings. Watch as you begin to perceive the darkness fade away as you bring your awareness to the light within yourself and others. Listen to your words as you start to offer expressions of acceptance and love to your friends and family. And when you quiet your mind, listen for Spirit to answer your calls for a miracle. Think about the connection between God and all of His Creations. And, remember always, that you are one with God, our Source of Light and Love. With Wisdom on your side, why would you be afraid of anything?

I love you and eagerly look forward to you joining me again as you read the next book in the series, *The Adventures of the Course Kids!*™. Check my website, ofcourse.com for the release date.

Love you always,
Barb

P.S. Remember the song that Faith said that she was writing for Grace? Well, you can now order the CD or download the MP3 version of *See with Your*

Heart by Barbara Franco Adams from Amazon.com and/or from cdbababy, at http://www.cdbaby.com/cd/barbarafrancoadams

P.P.S. Contact Barb Adams at barb@ofcoursepublishing.com with your comments and suggestions. Also, visit my website, ofcoursepublshing.com for ongoing insights, publication date of the next book in *The Adventures of the Course Kids!*™ series, and our developing list of Course Kids™ products!

Testimonials

"If you've ever looked for storybooks to help share your faith with your child, you know how hard they can be to find! *Through Faith and Grace* is a true-to-life story inviting children into Jesus' way of seeing the world. In the story, a parent and child experience a scary visit to a homeless shelter together and are transformed by the people. I can picture myself doing just that with my grandchildren after reading this book together! Barbara Franco Adams not only tells an appealing narrative, but she also provides valuable teaching techniques and follow-up questions to share with your child. Students of *A Course in Miracles* will be thrilled to find the core teachings in the story. I hope that she continues to write more stories! It is a gift that she has to both write and teach the teacher."

Rev. Mary Ramerman, B.A., M.A. Ed., M.A. Theology
Pastor Spiritus Christi Church, Rochester, NY

◇◇◇◇◇◇◇◇◇◇◇◇◇◇◇◇◇◇◇◇◇◇◇◇◇◇◇◇◇◇◇◇◇◇◇◇

"This is a heart-warming story of a young girl who learns the power of perception and how tuning in to God's reality changes everything she sees and feels. It opens her eyes to the Love that exists everywhere, and teaches her of the powerful results when she chooses to look with Love instead of fear."

Margaret Hannon-Holt, B.S.
Elementary Ed., M.S. Counselor, Ed., ACIM student

◇◇◇

"As a pediatrician, mother and student/teacher of both Eastern spiritual traditions and *A Course in Miracles*, I always seek materials that can teach powerful life lessons to younger audiences via the vehicle of entertainment. Those of us who work with younger tweens and teens on a regular basis know that many children have what can be referred to as 'selective hearing loss.' When we share what we think are priceless pearls of wisdom, they simply hear more 'adult blah-blah-blah.' Yet regardless of our age, we all savor a good story. In her first book, Barb Adams draws from her life as a mother, grandmother and educator to skillfully weave a beautiful story that reminded me of the importance of truly seeing with my heart rather than just my physical eyes. I enjoyed reading the first installment of the *Adventures of the Course Kids!*™ and look forward to many more to come. I recommend Barb's book to any adults seeking to share ACIM or simply as a more loving way to view life with the kids in their lives. "

Seema Khaneja, M.D.

Mother, ACIM/Eastern spirituality student and teacher

Acknowledgements

Thank you to all who love me and support me: My life partner, Roz Pullara, who offers her unconditional love. With the perspective of a writer and educator, she listens to and discusses my insights, and supports my spiritual journey through openness and discussion. My daughter Becky and son-in-law Greg, and my son and daughter-in-law, Luke and Jessica Adams who have been open to my travels on this journey, and who have encouraged me to pursue my life-goals. To my grandchildren Griffin, Emilia, Jacey and Sammy whose love fills me to the brim, and yet it overflows. To my children on Roz's side, Lisbeth and Chris Goossen, and Jen Pullara Blake who, by their actions allow me to be me and who opened their hearts and their minds to my pilgrimage. To my mother and father, Frances and Charles Franco, who loved me at full-throttle. To my sister Joan Franco Capuano, who first introduced me to *A Course in Miracles*. Joan continues to live her love for Jesus by extending it to me and all who cross her path. My brother Tom Franco and I have been on similar searches for peace and our paths have run parallel as we continue to revel in our discoveries and growth. His love has never been in question. To my college roommate and dear friend, Molly Scahill Yerdon for her unyielding support and love for me, and for introducing me to her family of origin, the fifteen-member Scahill clan. Parents, Tom and Bea Scahill were founding members of the St. Joseph's House of Hospitality in Rochester, NY, which was my inspiration for The Hospitality House. To my colleague and friend, Patricia Martin, former Director of Reading and ELA at the school district from which we retired, for assessing and determining the readability level of this book, for inspiring my love affair with literacy. To my friend and colleague, Anne Kramer, also a former Director of ELA helping with preliminary editing. To my spiritual mentor, guide, teacher and friend Patti Fields. After listening to Patti's homily at our church, which was rich in references to the Course, I knew that I had found my teacher. I am blessed to have her in my life. She willingly read my manuscript and offered insights and advice as the book unfolded. I'm forever grateful as she helps me find my way back to my true self. Finally, thank you to Roz and Angel who did the final editing.

With gratitude and love,
Barb

References to Lessons from
A Course in Miracles

Lessons that are integrated into *The Adventures of the Course Kids!™ Through Faith and Grace*:

*   *I have invented the world I see.* W-pI.32
*   *There is another way at looking at the world.* W-pI.33
*   *I am the Light of the world.* W-pI.61
*   *Miracles are seen in Light.* W-pI.91
*   *God's peace and joy are mine.* W-pI.105
*   *Let me be still and listen to the Truth.* W-pI.106
*   *Let me remember I am one with God.* W-pI.124
*   *All that I give is given to myself.* W-pI.126
*   *Now are we one with Him Who is our Source.* W-pI.164
*   *All fear is past and only love is here.* W-pII.293

References and Helpful Websites

A Course in Miracles Combined Volume, 2nd Edition, Foundation for Inner Peace, Viking, 1996.

Wapnick, Kenneth. *Absence from Felicity*, 2nd Edition. Foundation for Inner Peace, 1999.

Barbara Franco Adams .... ofcoursepublishing.com

Circle of Atonement .... circleofa.org

Miracle Distribution Center .... miraclecenter.org

Miracle Share .... miracleshare.org

Miracle Studies .... miraclestudies.net

Patti Fields-Barb's ACIM teacher and spiritual mentor .... pattifields.com

The Foundation for *A Course in Miracles* .... facim.org

The Foundation for Inner Peace .... acim.org

About the Author

Barbara Franco Adams is a retired educator with over 32 years of experience. As both a teacher and administrator, Barb was well respected by students, parents, and colleagues alike. At the height of her teaching career, she was selected as the *Teacher of the Year* by her state professional organization.

In 1996 Barb became acquainted with *A Course in Miracles* and started to study on her own. But in 2011, when she and her teacher were brought to each other, the Course truly spoke to Barb. Blending her career in education with her dedication to the teachings of the Course, Barb is developing a series for children, parents and caregivers. *The Adventures of the Course Kids!™ Through Faith and Grace* is the first in line.

Photo by Roz Pullara ©2014

Made in the USA
Monee, IL
18 November 2021

82493413R00038